Get Rich Action Plan

JAY TOMLINSON

PROJECTFREEMIND.COM

Copyright © 2016 Jay Tomlinson

All rights reserved.

ISBN: 1534634983
ISBN-13: 978-1534634985

CONTENTS

	Acknowledgments	i
	Introduction	iii.
1	Establish a Purpose	1
2	Slay the Beast Called Debt	7
3	Track Every Penny	15
4	Save, Baby, Save!	20
5	Invest the Surplus	26
6	The KISS Principle	30
7	Build the Snowball	37
8	Live Your Dreams	42
	Tools & Resources	44
	Special Bonus	45

ACKNOWLEDGMENTS

Thank you to my beta readers for making this book legible.

A special thanks to Julie and Darcy for catching all of my stupid mistakes.

JAY TOMLINSON

INTRODUCTION

Why I Wrote This Book

When I think back on my late teens and early 20's, I realize how little I was taught in high school and college about personal finance.

No one discussed at any stage of my young adult life the best practices to ensure financial success. No one warned me about the heavy burden of debt, the dangers of consumerism, or the perils of wage slavery.

I quickly realized I didn't want to spend 50 to 60 hours per week under someone else's control. I knew I had to find a way out that wouldn't take the next 40 years.

I am reminded of the lyrics of "Riders on the Storm" by The Doors, where Jim Morrison's powerful voice belts out, "Into this house we're born...into this world we're thrown." This chilling message ran through my head when I left the comforts of home for the first time at age 18. Four years later, I had a degree in business, but I still had no clue about personal finance outside of the standard advice. I was thrown into the real world with very little real world knowledge.

I realized I needed to educate myself about personal finance, and what I learned was *entirely* different from anything I ever learned in school or from the media.

I poured through countless personal finance books and blogs, and I sifted through a LOT of backwards advice from the so-called experts. I took everything I learned and formulated a simple strategy that anyone can use to achieve financial freedom much quicker than the standard advice would suggest. The result of that strategy is the simple 8-step action plan I cover in this book.

I created the 8 steps to work regardless of income level. The most I have ever made in a year was $60,000 before taxes. Most of the time I make a lot less. But I do whatever it takes to keep building my net worth so I can live life on my terms. At the age of 28 I quit my job to travel for four months. Now I spend my time growing my online business instead of on the clock, all because I implemented those 8 steps early in my career and made smart financial decisions.

I now don't have to worry about making money for years to come, and I don't plan on going back to a full-time job any time soon. That's because I have the right systems in place and the right mindset to build and preserve my wealth in both good times and bad.

The media will have you believe that unless you're a multi-millionaire, the best you can do is save 10% and retire at 65. Nonsense!

The game has changed. The old wisdom has become obsolete. I needed to write a book calling B.S. on the old advice to prove that you *can* take control of your finances and your life right now, and you can do it at a *much* faster pace.

You don't have to toil away for the next 40 years so you can enjoy your last 20. Once I realized this truth, I knew I needed to share it. Life is too short to waste it feeling uninspired and powerless.

The big banks and financial institutions thrive on uncertainty, so of course they want you to think managing your money is complicated. They *want* you to think 40 years of work is necessary in order to "have enough." I'm here to tell you it's simply not true. Establishing the right habits early and sticking with them will cause a snowball effect that generates a lifetime of wealth. This simple guide shows you how to do it.

Each of the 8 action steps can be implemented within a month or less. It usually takes at least 30 days to develop a habit, and some of these steps may require habit changes that will take some time to implement.

I'm not going to lie and say it's *easy* to change lifelong habits, but the advice itself is not rocket science. Old habits die hard, but after reading this book, you will have everything laid out for you, and you will know what needs to be done. If you make financial freedom a priority, you *will* succeed.

Trust me – if I have the will power to learn and implement these steps, so can you!

By writing this book, I hope to drastically reduce that learning curve so anyone can take the fast road to financial independence with just a few life changes. Everything you need is included in this book. The key is taking action!

* * *

Why You Should Read This Book

Every financial decision you make in your life has a major impact on your future. You might be paying for college or entering the work force for the first time, Either way, it is imperative you get started on the right foot.

Whether you are in your 20's and looking for sound advice to get started or you're in your 30's and realized you never really thought about financial freedom, it's never too late!

Time is the greatest asset you have when dealing with money; the more time you have, the easier it is to grow your wealth. That's why it's important to start as soon as possible!

I'm here to show you the importance of getting it right today so that you don't have to worry about it 40 years from now. If you take this guide to heart, you will realize that retirement at 65 should NOT be the norm, and you can realize financial independence in your 30's or 40's.

This book is broken into 8 chapters, each an actionable step on the road to financial freedom. Depending on your current life situation, some of the information in Chapter 2 about college or student loans might not apply to you, but all 8 chapters contain essential action steps for achieving financial freedom in a short period of time.

Each chapter is full of strategies, tips and tricks to achieve that particular step. At the end of each chapter, I will summarize the key takeaways and give you a plan of action. As an added bonus, you also receive a link to my free guide, "27 Ways I Slashed My Budget by $1818 per Month." Implementing the strategies in this book and in the free guide will save you tens of thousands, if not hundreds of thousands of dollars over your lifetime!

I'm here to show you it's not rocket science. It just requires the commitment and dedication to make some lifestyle changes that will pay dividends (literally!) for years to come.

You made the right choice picking up this book, and you have shown that you're serious about your money. The first step of learning something new and different can be a difficult one to take. The next and *most* difficult step is implementing what you learn.

I am confident after you read this book you will have the knowledge and resources necessary to steer yourself toward financial independence and freedom.

So let's get started!

JAY TOMLINSON

1 ESTABLISH A PURPOSE

Oh no, not another feel-good self help book! Don't worry, the title of this chapter is not meant to invoke images of motivational speakers, but the truth is that purpose means everything!

We all have a reason for being here, even if it doesn't always feel that way. Whether life has an inherent meaning or not, we all have the freedom of choice to create a life that we truly want! It just takes some thought and introspection. That is what this chapter is all about.

Before we get into the nitty gritty of finances, it's imperative to take the time to reflect on your life purpose.

My Story

One year or so into my 9 to 5 existence in the corporate world, something clicked. Maybe it was the dreaded alarm clock going off before I was ready to start the day. Maybe it was the water cooler talk at the office about last night's episode of "Dancing with the Stars." Maybe it was the work assignment that left me feeling stressed and uninspired.

Whatever the reason, I realized I could not continue this lifestyle for the next 40 years.

I was working in Corporate America, doing what society told me I was supposed to do. It didn't feel right.

This discontent left me wondering what was wrong with me. *Why am I so unhappy if I'm doing everything right? I went to college, got a job, and now I work in a cubicle just like everyone else.*

That's when it hit me; there is no one right way to live. Sure, I was raised to think this was the way to go, but it doesn't have to be that way.

So I took action. I thought long and hard about what I really wanted to do and I kept taking steps in that direction. Before you can start thinking about mastering your finances, you need to know *why* you want financial freedom. You need a purpose. That's what this chapter is all about.

What's Your Story?

Maybe you love your job. You feel you make a difference and you can't wait to get to work every morning. If so, that's great! You are very fortunate to have found your calling and it sounds like you already know your life purpose. Even if you are in this boat, keep reading! Defining your purpose and your goals is a continuous process.

If you feel in any way how I felt when working for the Man, this chapter will resonate even more. You feel something is missing in your life or you are not spending a large percentage of your day doing what you want to do.

So many of us go through the motions each day because we feel trapped. And in many cases, we *are* trapped because we have built an unsustainable way of life that requires us to toil at an unfulfilling job in order to support the lifestyle we have created. This vicious cycle is the reason most people work well into their 60's. Not because they want to, but because they *have* to.

I'm here to yell a resounding *NO*! You don't have to live this way!

You can drastically reduce the percentage of your life spent working at something you hate if you take some time to define your life purpose.

You are self-aware enough to realize you don't want to continue on your current path, and you are reading this book. So you obviously want to make a change!

If you know what you want out of life, you will realize the importance of financial success and you will live *deliberately* and spend your time wisely.

Remember, we only get one life and a finite amount of time! Why spend it wandering aimlessly or worse yet, doing what you already know you don't want to do?

What Do You Want 5 Years From Now?

This is a loaded question and one that I am constantly revising. The reason I like to think of 5-year goals instead of longer term is because our dreams and goals change all the time.

When I was in college, my five-year goal was to make a six figure salary as a manager in an accounting firm. Fast forward to today, and I have no desire to ever reach that status!

If your goal is to climb the corporate ladder and make lots of money, that's great! I applaud you for your ambition. (It's not for everyone though, so don't think you are stuck!)

Understanding what you want five years from now is a vital beginning step on the road to financial freedom. When I sat down and really thought out what I wanted my life to be, I realized I had no use for the amount of money or stress my field of work would bring. My lifestyle would not improve by compounding my stress just to make more money.

Of course, money is great. I wouldn't be writing this book if I didn't love the peace of mind and options it can bring. But the old adage "money can't buy happiness" is also true. Knowing how much is enough for you will improve your life in so many ways and help you avoid chasing that dangling carrot the rest of your life.

Writing Out Your Goals

Again, all of our goals are different, so be sure to ask yourself the question "what are my goals for five years from now?" and really think about it. Lock yourself in a quiet room with no distractions and just start writing it out.

Don't worry about grammar or spelling. Just write from your stream of consciousness everything that comes to mind. Step away from it for a bit and later you can look at everything you wrote to edit it into something meaningful and focused.

In my case, I realized in my mid-20's that my five year goal was to start a location independent business so I could have the freedom to travel the world. I currently have a paragraph written out that looks like this:

"In five years, I will have built a sustainable online business utilizing multiple income streams, which will allow me to live from anywhere in the world through the use of e-commerce, book publishing, and Internet marketing, all with the purpose of creating value in areas where I have knowledge and interest. As a result of my efforts, I will have the free time to travel, volunteer, and further pursue my interests and passions while generating passive income."

Every year, I look back at this paragraph and tweak it depending on my current situation. Once I am generating the level of income I am seeking, my five-year goal will include less about making money and more about pursuing my true passions.

Maybe your goal includes building ties to your community and raising a family. Maybe in five years you will be early in your career and want to move to a city that is booming with opportunities in your field.

Whatever you want to accomplish, try to be specific, but understand that even five year goals can change. If you know yourself and know what you want, working toward financial freedom will become a no brainer!

Choosing Your Goals Wisely

I should also emphasize that the age-old advice to "follow your passion" can be dangerous if you are serious about financial success.

One of my passions is wilderness backpacking. It would be great if I could make a living walking through the woods every day, but unfortunately wilderness jobs are very competitive with mostly low wage positions. Maybe I should have ignored all of that and gone for it, but I decided on a different career path that would pay more and bring me financial freedom at a faster pace.

Remember, this is all about maximizing how much free time you have on this planet, because time is the most precious resource we have!

On a side note, if you don't have your career path figured out yet, don't worry! In fact, I find it ridiculous that at the age of 18 and with minimal real world experience, we are expected to know what we want to do the rest of our lives.

I still don't know exactly what I want from life, but by writing everything down I am taking steps toward what I *do* know I want. The younger you are, the more difficult it will be to figure out your goals, but the great news is that you have your whole life ahead of you!

Our most valuable resource is time, and the more time you have, the more you can afford to make mistakes. After all, we learn the most from our mistakes, so don't be afraid to take a chance on yourself. *You only fail when you don't try!*

Maybe college isn't for you, which is perfectly fine! In fact, with the absurdly high cost of tuition these days, I would advise my 18 year old self to work in a skilled trade after high school or take a year off to travel if circumstances allow.

The choices for how to live your life are endless, so don't let anyone force you one way or the other. The key is writing down your goals and taking action!

How Much Do You Really Need to Achieve Your Goals?

One of the reasons you need to clearly define your life purpose and 5-year goals is to realize how *little* you need in order to be happy.

Unless your dreams involve living in a 20,000 square foot mansion, you do not need to make millions of dollars to find success. My guess is that after you went through the exercise above and really thought about your goals, you realized you don't need as much as you once thought.

You might still think you need that Lamborghini or large estate, but I'm here to tell you that you don't.

Studies have consistently shown that after a certain level of income, happiness does not increase. Not only that, you're most likely wasting the best years of your life working for those things that ultimately you'll either never get, or they won't make you happy.

So throw away your preconceived notions that "success = millions of dollars." The reason successful people seem happier is because they know their life purpose and they are doing a really good job at delivering on that purpose. In other words, they are happy because they are successful at achieving their goals. That is why they are so wealthy!

But it isn't the wealth that makes rich people happy; it is the validation that their life purpose is adding value to the world by creating wealth. See the difference? There are plenty of miserable rich people too!

Most likely, if you really thought about the first step in this chapter and what you want from life, you will see it doesn't need to cost much. Even if it involves travel, there are very affordable and fun ways to see the world that don't involve staying at the most expensive resorts.

Throughout this book, I will show you how easy and fun saving money can be in all aspects of your life. My hope is your whole mindset about spending money will change!

As human beings, we are driven toward helping one another. It is in our DNA to want to give to those in need. I believe it is this ambition to help others and add value that really makes us happy. If that is your mindset, you will soon realize how *little* you need and how few material possessions you require to be happy.

Once your basic needs are met, you can focus all of your efforts on making yourself a better person and the world around you a better place. With this attitude, you will quickly find your wealth compounding into more than you could ever possibly need!

Key Takeaways

Whether your purpose comes through your job, volunteer work, or your family, you will find that what truly brings happiness does not require "keeping up with the Joneses." It only requires fighting for what you believe and going after what really makes you tick.

By spending some quiet time thinking through your goals and desires and writing them out, you should have a pretty good idea of what path you want to take. You only get one chance on this planet, so it's imperative to create a purpose to make the most of your time here!

Finish a rough version of your goals before moving on to any other action steps in this book. You should have some kind of life philosophy and direction you want to take yourself before you start thinking about the more detailed aspects of personal finance. You only get one shot at life, so try to envision what you want it to look like before you put in a bunch of effort getting there!

Now that you have taken the time to think through your goals, you are well on your way to the life you always envisioned! The next step involves digging into the specifics of starting down the right path toward financial freedom!

2 SLAY THE BEAST CALLED DEBT

As many of you already know, the United States economy is built on debt. Just look at the current U.S. government national debt numbers and you'll see what I mean!

This debt economy carries down to us as consumers and has turned into a way of life for many of us. With the accessibility of credit cards, mortgages, and student loans, it's no wonder that we're all in debt!

We are groomed from day 1 to think debt is perfectly normal and healthy, but it's not!

Debt is a form of slavery, and I don't consider that to be hyperbole.

Think about it: as long as you are in debt, you have to work against your will. You owe your time and effort to someone else just to live. Once you come to this realization, you will do everything in your power to never owe money again!

Obviously, real life happens and you will most likely take out some kind of loan at some point, whether it's for college, buying a house, whatever the case may be. But guess what? If you're smart about it you will never have to be a slave to someone else.

Keep reading to see what I mean.

You Don't Have To Go To College!

I think it's unfortunate that most high school counselors and parents push their kids toward college even if it isn't right for them. And with the cost of tuition climbing each year, it's becoming more and more unrealistic to take on those costs. Something has to give, and it's not going to be the financial institutions. It's going to be you, the little guy. Sorry to be so blunt, but that's how it works.

That said, I am not vehemently opposed to getting a college degree. It can prove invaluable over the course of your career, assuming you choose a marketable major. I have a degree and it has afforded me some great opportunities. I was fortunate enough to receive financial aid that made the burden much less than it is on many of my peers.

If you are reading this in your teenage years and/or you haven't started college yet, I'm thrilled that you're studying personal finance at such a young age! So here's my advice to you: Think long and hard about whether you really *need* to go to college to achieve the goals and dreams you outlined in Chapter 1.

Many times, you simply have no other choice but to get that four-year degree for the field you want to pursue, but if you dig a little deeper into your career field, you may find that an associate's degree or some classes at a community college are more than enough education.

Or, you might be able to get to work right now and gain experience through an actual job. Imagine that!

Let me tell you a secret: humans aren't designed to sit in front of a professor and look at PowerPoint slides for four years. That is not the best use of our time. We learn by doing.

If there is any way at all for you to find work in your field of interest right away, go for it! You will learn more *and* get paid. It's a win-win.

The Bureau of Labor Statistics (http://www.bls.gov/ooh) is an invaluable resource for researching job outlooks and education requirements in every single industry. Use this free resource to your advantage to see if your career aspirations will easily land you a job. If you need years and years of education (i.e. years and years of debt) to get anywhere in your field, you might want to reconsider.

If college is a necessity to get ahead, consider working first then going to school while you work. There are many companies who will even pay your way through college. Do whatever it takes to slay that beast called debt as soon possible!

Even if the job you have while in college does not relate to your major, you will most likely learn just as much in whatever job you find as you do in a classroom.

No matter the job, you will get to see how a business operates rather than just reading about it in a textbook. I learned just as much about business in four months as a restaurant cook than I did in four years as a student!

* * *

Student Loans: The Ugliest Beast of All

I consider student loans to be the "sirens" of debt. In the classic novel *The Odyssey*, the sirens tempted Odysseus and his crew toward their island with their enchanting music and voices. In the same way, the higher education establishment tempts juniors and seniors in high school with promises of the best years of their life and a world of riches after graduation.

I have many fond memories of my days in college and wouldn't trade them for anything, but the reality is that college is not for everyone, and if it that siren song tempts you in the wrong direction, you will soon find yourself digging your way out of a hole for the rest of your career.

Minimize the Damage

Student loans are a real treat. For the privilege of learning, you find yourself in a massive, steaming pile of debt that takes years to pay off. All politics aside, suffice it to say that student loans have become a huge problem in the United States and they aren't going to magically go away. Maybe we'll see a drastic change as a result of economic events, but either way someone has to pay. If the 2008 bailout is any indication, it's not going to be the banks. It's going to be you!

If you haven't started college yet and are dead set on going, please please *please* look at the cost of tuition for each school you are interested in attending and apply for every possible scholarship you can.

The difference in costs between attending a state school and a private school can be astronomical. One mistake I made was not thinking enough about those costs. I was young and knew nothing about personal finance.

Sit down with your parents or someone you trust and really look at what your 4-year commitment is going to cost you at each of the schools you are considering. I cannot stress this enough!

Debt has a snowball effect, and every dollar matters. I am not saying go to the absolute cheapest place you can find – depending on your major, that could be a huge mistake. But most public universities are far more inexpensive and just as prestigious as their private counterparts.

Don't fall into the trap of going to a school because of the name and "prestige" unless you really need that name to make it in your career. (And if your career is that competitive, I would suggest rereading Chapter 1 and choosing a different path. I'm of the opinion that each of us has multiple passions and talents, some more practical than others, but that's a topic for another time.)

Student loans usually have pretty favorable interest rates; I consider anything less than 5% pretty good. And in many cases the interest can get paid off if it's subsidized. The problem is there are limits on how much is subsidized, and you could end up with six figures in loans, depending on how much you need for your four year degree. That will take years or even decades of full time work to pay off.

It is getting more and more difficult to justify the price tag on a four year degree, no matter how you look at it. Is it really worth hundreds of thousands of dollars and years of debt?

Should You Take the Road Less Traveled?

Carefully assess your situation and how much debt you are liable to assume before jumping into a 4-year undergraduate program. You might have second thoughts and decide to enter a skilled trade instead. There is no shame in sticking it to the education system and avoiding the massive hole you will dig for yourself with a student loan. While all of your peers are paying into the system and massively in debt, you will be *making* money and well on your way to financial independence.

Of course, many entry level jobs after college will pay a lot more than what a blue collar apprentice could make out of high school. And if you have a good scholarship and are entering a high paying field (e.g. STEM jobs), college could very well be worth it in the long run.

Just make sure to think long and hard about this decision; I am probably beating a dead horse by now, but I can't stress it enough! The right financial decisions today will make a world of difference tomorrow. (In other words, if you decide to spend $200,000 plus interest for a degree in underwater basket weaving, you're probably going to regret it in the near future.)

Credit Cards: The Good, the Bad, and the Ugly

Credit cards are a very dangerous game. But I have a confession to make: I own several of them. If you pay them off and build your credit score, credit cards are amazing! If you don't, they turn into a beast that can grow to be even uglier than student loans!

I have seen fortunes vanish from credit card debt, and with the easy access to credit in today's world, it's a simple trap to fall into. Credit card companies prey on college students and young professionals.

How do you think they make money? They target those of us who are the most financially vulnerable and charge 20 or even 30% interest if we don't pay on time! It's absurd, but it works.

Treat Credit Like Cash

The key take away from the insanity of high interest credit cards is to never buy what you can't afford with cash. Seems simple, right?

If you couldn't go to your ATM and get enough money to pay for that cool new gadget, don't use your credit card to pay for it! When it comes time to pay the piper, you may not have the funds to cover that expense, and the credit card company will gladly tack on 25 or 30 cents for every dollar on your balance. And guess what? They'll be nice enough to compound that amount next month!

So the $1.25 you owe becomes $1.56 on the next statement, then $1.95, and so on! Assume that dollar is actually $10,000 and you'll see what I mean about the path of destruction credit cards can leave. It only takes a few months for that $10,000 balance to double! You are effectively paying twice as much for goods than you would have had you paid in cash.

With all of those ominous disclaimers out of the way, credit cards can also work wonders for you financially if you avoid their traps. Many of them have excellent sign on bonuses and rewards for using them.

Check out NerdWallet.com for some of the best credit cards for your situation. I recommend for those just establishing credit to find a card with no annual fee.

I pay for everything with my credit card if I'm able because I often get 5% cash back or points toward travel. But that's because I have the money in the bank to cover the expenses I pay! (Beware though that rewards programs are also a ploy to get you to spend more money so you can capture those great perks! Don't feel like you need to spend more money just to get more rewards.)

The more you use and pay off credit cards, the better your credit. The better your credit, the more you qualify for better credit cards and more favorable loans.

Depending on how you manage your credit cards, you will find yourself on either a virtuous or vicious cycle. The choice is yours!

The Home Mortgage: Is It the American Dream?

Let's face it: if you plan to live somewhere for a long period of time and/or raise a family, you will probably need to buy a home at some point in your life. And with that comes a mortgage.

Rent or Own?

If you are just starting your career, I would advise finding a rental, especially if you don't have a family yet. Odds are, you probably won't have much credit established anyway, so you're not going to find any favorable mortgage terms.

It is much easier to take on a year lease in an apartment or rental home than it is to commit to owning a house. So think long and hard before buying.

Depending on your city, Craigslist and simply driving around are usually enough to find plenty of places to rent. Don't be afraid to split costs with roommates, either. The savings will be huge. And find a place to live that is close to your work or school! There is no bigger money and time sink than the long commute.

The New York Times has a cool Rent vs. Own calculator (http://nyti.ms/1jHOBkp) if you aren't sure which route to take. Most likely, you will want to rent if you are in your 20's and don't have a family yet.

Choosing What's Best for You

I don't want to get into much specifics about mortgages and home ownership, just a little philosophy about housing in general. So bear with me while I get on my soapbox.

Mortgages can be an affordable form of debt with an asset to show for it in the end. But I would *never* recommend going after the McMansion and buying more than you need. Why get a five bedroom, four bathroom palace if it's just you and your significant other?

Every square foot you buy is another square foot of not only up-front cost, but cost to maintain, heat, cool, and clean. Not only that, we feel the need to fill up all these extra rooms with more stuff we can't afford.

It's time to rethink how much space is really necessary for a place to live. The average U.S. house size has reached 2,600 square feet, about 1,100 square feet larger than 30 years ago! At what size will we stop and say enough is enough?

Take your time finding the right living situation for you and try to rethink the standard advice of more is better. Remember that happiness does not come from owning more junk.

Saving on Housing Costs

Since housing will be your biggest expense over your lifetime, do whatever you can to slash that cost.

If you own your home and have any spare bedrooms, explore the option of renting them out. You could also use Airbnb.com to rent out your home whenever you can afford to leave the house for a while. Any way you are able to reduce monthly housing costs, go for it.

If you rent, look for a studio or share a house or apartment with roommates. You will save thousands of dollars per year doing this.

Housing is Not an Investment

One final note on housing: I do not consider owning a house an "investment" like many people do, although it certainly can be if you know what you're doing. For the most part I would consider a house a depreciable asset like almost anything else you buy.

That being said, as long as you do your research, buy in a desirable location, and don't neglect your property, the odds are you will own something of considerable value that will hopefully hold its worth over time. In other words, you won't be losing your shirt when it's all said and done like you will with a student loan.

Key Takeaways

If you take away one key point from this chapter, it's that everyone wants your money! It's true. That's how the world works. You can either fall into the trap or walk around it.

Don't let the establishment force you into thinking you need to take out that huge loan for college, and don't let them fool you into thinking you need all those expensive toys so you become a slave to credit. If you find yourself with any debt whatsoever, you need to tackle it right now!

So here's what you do: after paying for all your necessary expenses for the month (rent, groceries, etc.) look at your interest rates, and pay off the highest rate *first* with whatever amount of money you have left over.

If you have credit card debt charging you 25% interest, pay off as much of it as you can first before you tackle any other interest.

Most likely your credit card rate will be the highest. Next is probably student loans. Pay off as much of these debts as you can as fast as you can. But don't bite off more than you can chew! Only pay off what you can afford to pay.

At this point, you might be thinking, "No sh*t, Sherlock." But the simplest advice is usually the best advice. And despite how common sense it seems, the U.S. continues to operate on a mountain of debt.

It might take a few months of paying your bills before you figure out a comfortable balance of how much you should pay off each month. The key is starting now by taking the largest chunk possible out of your next statement. Just don't bite off more than you can chew. As you implement the savings advice later in this book, you'll be able to pay off these balances at a faster and faster pace every time they come due.

Remember: if you can't afford it, you probably don't need it. Just because you earn $75,000 per year doesn't mean you need to spend that and then some.

If you don't earn anything, you're going to have to make sacrifices. There is no shame in it. I lived in poverty during my college years and had some of the best times of my life. The point being you will quickly learn to make do with what you have. You will adapt to your frugal lifestyle and realize how little you need to be happy.

Finally, you may have a mortgage charging a fixed 4 or 5% interest rate. Honestly, you will be fine paying off this mortgage over 30 years or whatever your term happens to be, assuming you have a low rate.

I like to use 5% as a baseline. Anything higher than that I consider expensive debt and anything lower I consider cheap. On average, you can earn 8% on the stock market, so I find 5% to be pretty reasonable. That being said, if you abhor debt as much as I do and have the funds to pay it off quicker, by all means do so!

There are obviously other debt instruments besides these three, such as auto loans or business loans. I would advise keeping your auto loan as small as possible by buying an inexpensive used car, which I will discuss in a later chapter.

I am a huge fan of entrepreneurship and starting your own business, especially if it means you can avoid working for the man! But if you need a business loan for it, you obviously need to understand the risk. I personally never use debt as leverage, for businesses, investing, or otherwise. Consider lower cost ventures instead. There are plenty of online businesses you can start for $100 or less!

Okay, enough about debt. Just remember these words and repeat them to yourself whenever tempted to borrow money now to sacrifice freedom later: Debt it is the opposite of freedom. It is legalized slavery! It is a beast that must be slain as soon as humanly possible.

3 TRACK EVERY PENNY

Now that you have an idea of the direction you want to take your life and you have a plan for managing your debt, it's time to look at your expenses.

This chapter covers some of my favorite aspects of finance; managing expenses is one of the most powerful ways to reach financial independence at a young age. Sure, making millions of dollars per year also helps, but not all of us are that lucky.

The single greatest tool you have as a consumer is choice. There are so many options for how to spend money it's overwhelming. You can choose to spend your hard earned dollars on all the high tech shiny gadgets that are thrown in front of you or you can choose to live on less.

No one is forcing you to buy all of this stuff. The classic quote from *Fight Club* rings true: "The things you own end up owning you."

This chapter will go over some powerful ways to minimize your expenses and outline exactly what you can do to avoid modern society's overpowering consumer trap.

How to Track Where Your Money is Going

Monitoring expenses is absolutely vital to financial success. If you were to take away just *one* thing from this book, I would say looking at your expenses each month is the number one habit you should form.

You *have* to know where every dollar goes and. you *must* implement a system to track it all if you are serious about financial freedom. The good news is that plenty of software already exists that will do exactly that, and some options are even free!

Mint

Mint.com is a web-based software that logs all of your financial transactions and allows you to create budgets, view charts and graphs of your expenses and investments, and more. This is my software of choice, and it's completely free! It takes all of the guess work out of your finances by connecting directly with your bank accounts, credit cards, and investment accounts to give you a full picture of your financial health.

Mint will automatically download all of your financial transactions for the account you link and attempt to categorize them (e.g. paycheck, housing, food, entertainment, etc.) It's as easy as heading to Mint and creating an account, then adding all of your financial accounts into the system.

Most financial accounts are supported by Mint, although I have had some connectivity issues with certain accounts. That being said, they continue to improve and are hands down the best free option for personal finance software.

Of course, if you are paying for items in cash, you will need to manually enter these transactions into Mint. I would strongly suggest you get into the habit of logging *every* transaction into Mint, regardless of dollar amount. Those $2 and $3 cash transactions add up fast! If you are going to Starbucks every day and paying cash, you could be blowing $100 to $200 per month without even thinking twice about it. Log *everything* and inspect *everything*. Your freedom depends on it!

Note: Some people are concerned with the security of Mint as it requires you to enter all of your account information into one centralized location. This is a legitimate concern. However, the security of Mint, is comparable to any online banking system. The company is owned by Intuit, the same company that owns Quicken and TurboTax, which have a great reputation.

You Need A Budget (YNAB)

Another option for tracking expenses is You Need A Budget (ynab.com). I have personally never used this program but have heard great things. It does cost money for a subscription, but you can try it for free for a month.

If you're a college student, you can get YNAB for free! Follow these steps to get a free copy (http://bit.ly/1RGI8pB).

Microsoft Excel

You could track every single expense transaction on a spreadsheet manually. But that gets very tedious very fast. I would not recommend doing this considering the automated options available today. The one benefit of Excel is that keying in your transactions will make you that much more aware of your spending. Since Mint does most of the work for you, it's a little more hands off than keying everything in yourself.

If you spend cash for everything, you will need to manually track expenses and either Excel or Google Sheets will be your best bet. The great benefit of Google Sheets is that your files are stored in the Cloud and can be accessed anywhere you have an Internet connection.

You could also track everything in Mint and import into Excel or Sheets for further analysis depending on how detailed you want to get. On your "Transactions" page in Mint, you will see an Export link at the bottom of the page to export as a comma separated (CSV) file. Sometimes I will export expense transactions from Mint into Excel for the past twelve months just to see percent changes in certain categories over time.

Creating a Budget and Reviewing Your Expenses

Using the power of Mint or YNAB, you can easily create budgets for yourself and track expenses by category. The tools are all there and very straightforward; it's just a matter of putting them into use.

In Mint, simply click the "Budgets" link, where you can create budgets for any and all spending categories, along with a budget of what you expect income to be on a monthly basis. Once you have everything budgeted, you'll be able to easily tell how much you are expecting to save (or lose) each month. Your budget will compare these to what you have actually spent in each category based on transaction detail from your credit cards.

Each month, you can review your expenses against your budget and see where you are doing better and worse than expected. As more and more data gets tracked in Mint, you will have a clearer picture of where your money is going and you can adjust your budget as necessary.

You will also start to realize where you are spending way too much and you can focus on cutting those costs. Set up a reminder in your calendar on the first of each month to review previous month expenses in Mint. I like to use Google Calendar to set up recurring reminders for tasks like this.

Note: Mint has to "guess" what category to place all of the transactions it downloads off your credit cards, and it's not always right. I like to skim through the Transactions page once a month and re-categorize everything that needs fixed. This will give you a much more accurate picture of your expenses versus your budget.

Major Categories

Normally the largest categories in a budget are Income, Housing, Food, Transportation, Entertainment, Education, Clothing, and Healthcare. The great thing about Mint is that it already has these categories set up, and it will attempt to guess where each of your expense transactions falls.

I have already covered housing and education costs in the previous chapter. In later chapters, I will go into more detail on cost cutting for the rest of these expense categories, so stay tuned! Soon your finances will be a well-oiled wealth-building machine.

Do You Really Need a Budget?

Almost anything you read about personal finance will tell you the importance of a budget. I tend to agree, but it also depends on your situation.

If you fall in line with the average American and spend close to or more than what you earn, then you absolutely need a budget to get your finances in order. However, a lot of financial advice seems to be, "Create a budget so you can spend every single dollar you make and not a penny less!"

Maybe that's exaggerating a bit, but budgets are often created by taking your income and then filling every dollar of that income with an expense when that's the wrong way to look at it. If you take home $10,000 per month, should you creatively think of ways to spend as much of those $10,000 as possible? If you ask me, hell no! That's a wasteful way to live. If you make that much, sure you can afford to be a little more loose with your money, but don't fall into the trap of thinking you should spend it all because your budget says you can.

Remember, you work hard for your money. Is it worth it to you to blow it all so that you have to work even harder in the future?

It's all about needs versus wants. Which expenses do you need in order to live and which are luxuries? Is spending $1,000 per month on the latest gadgets really making you happy when your old gadgets work perfectly fine?

Once you understand what you *need* as opposed to what you *want*, a budget will become less and less necessary. You will find yourself buying less and less and not needing to refer to a budget when it's time to make a purchase. Your whole mentality of buying things will change and you'll be saving more and more each month!

Key Takeaways

You *must* keep track of income and expenses if you're serious about financial freedom. Get on Mint, get on You Need a Budget, or use Excel. Do whatever it takes to track it all. Once you start tracking everything, you will automatically make more conscious decisions every time you take out that credit card or wad of cash.

Once you start using the right tool for you to keep track of your finances, you can set up budgets to rein in your spending. Then you will begin to transform the way you think about spending and you won't even need to budget. That's because you will find yourself analyzing every financial transaction you make when it happens. And you'll find that your bank account will be growing month after month!

Keep in mind that old saying, "A penny saved is a penny earned." You've probably heard that phrase one too many times in your life, but it's absolutely true. In a later chapter, I'll show you the amazing power of savings and investments and how essential it is to invest at a young age. By controlling your spending, you will continue to increase your savings and your financial health will snowball into something truly amazing!

4 SAVE, BABY, SAVE!

You're making an income, you're living in an affordable home, and you're tracking your expenses through Mint or some other software. Now what? Now it's time to cut the fat!

The truth is that trimming expenses is a lifelong commitment that can always be improved. And it's a ton of fun once you start working that frugality muscle and noticing huge increases in your net worth!

This chapter will show some great ways to cut on everyday expenses. It starts with the right philosophy on needs versus wants covered in the previous chapter, and by realizing you can live a great life on a fraction of the cost.

Food

This category will vary wildly from person to person depending on your habits. While there are many great ways to cut costs on food, I would not recommend anyone live on Ramen noodles just to get that number down. Your health is the most important asset you have, so do *not* sacrifice that just to increase your net worth a few bucks. In the long run, the medical bills and lower quality of life will end up costing you a lot more.

There are so many diets out there that I will not get into all of that – just listen to your body and eat what makes you feel good. *Then* focus on cutting costs for those staples you buy every week.

There are plenty of ways to cut down on your food bill. The most obvious one is eating at home. If you don't know how to cook, teach yourself right now!

Eating out every day is a huge drain on your budget. If you're spending

$100 per week eating out for lunch and dinner, that's over $5000 per year! You can easily make yourself a $3 salad that would cost $12 at the nearby lunch spot. All of these costs add up to astronomical amounts when you stop and think about it.

There's nothing wrong with treating yourself once in a while, but it should be just that – a treat! Going out to dinner loses its excitement pretty quickly when you're already doing it a few times a week.

And don't be afraid to say, "No thanks" to your work buddies who want to eat out for lunch every day. Camaraderie is important, but you can do that in other ways. Tell them you're saving money or you're on a special diet and I'm sure they'll understand. If they don't, maybe it's time to find new friends.

If you can read directions, you can cook. You will save so much money and eat so much healthier at a fraction of the cost, not to mention the satisfaction of not feeling helpless when it comes time to feed yourself.

Whether you prepare meals for the whole week and freeze them for later or prepare them each day – do whatever you find easiest to get yourself in the habit of making your own food. You *must* learn to prepare food for yourself.

Constantly be on the lookout for the lowest cost options for staples in your diet, and always consider lower cost substitutes. Do you need that cheese for $20 a pound when the one for $4 a pound is just as good?

If you have an Aldi grocery store near you, go to it! Their prices are insanely cheap. You may also want to consider buying in bulk at wholesale clubs. Also, buy in season – fruits and vegetables that are in season are cheaper and they're often local. While we're on the topic of fruits and vegetables, if you're eating a lot of them and have the room, why not grow your own?

Transportation

I'm about to tell you about this amazing new technology called *the Internet* that has opened up the lines of communication for everyone and made it extremely easy to compare prices when buying products. You don't have to drive from store to store to find the best price – you can do it all online! And when making a huge purchase like a vehicle, comparing prices is extremely important.

I would strongly advise against buying a new car. That $30,000 car you're eyeballing is just a consumable good. That's it. So what if it looks cool? Ten years from now when that expensive piece of metal is in a scrap yard, will it really matter?

Most likely, you just need something moderately comfortable to get you from point A to point B. So do yourself a favor and save several thousand dollars by buying used. Scour Craigslist or better yet, AutoTempest.com, which compiles used cars available from numerous sources.

Look at local auctions. Find an honest used car dealer (believe it or not, they do exist). There are so many perfectly good used cars out there just waiting to be driven!

While we're on the topic of Craigslist, get on there and look for a good used bike! Why burn fuel for those short trips into town when you can cruise around on a bike and get in shape in the process? It will more than pay for itself in reduced fuel costs and improved health.

As I mentioned in a previous chapter, cut down on your commute and you will see huge savings in transportation costs. Live close to work or find a new job closer to home. Take the bus if you can. Or look for gigs that will allow you to work from home.

Assuming gas plus the wear and tear on your car comes out to about $0.50 per mile, that means you're spending $25 per day if you have a round trip commute of 50 miles, not to mention the time it takes to make that drive. So if your job pays $25 per hour, you're basically working an hour per day just to pay for your commute! That's money down the drain.

Entertainment

We live in a culture that constantly requires stimulation and excitement. There's nothing wrong with entertainment, but maybe it's time to consider getting it from different sources.

Instead of that huge monthly cable bill, cut the cord and go with Netflix. Instead of paying $50 a month to watch commercials, you're now spending less than $10 for on demand commercial free content. Sounds like a good deal to me.

You might think you need to have cable to get the sports channels, but if you really *must* watch your favorite teams in action, there are plenty of other ways (some legitimate and some not so much).

It also wouldn't hurt to replace all that TV time with a more productive hobby, like getting a library card and reading books for free! Trust me – if you give up cable, you will not miss it. I don't know of anyone who has regretted cutting cable. Your peace of mind will improve dramatically by removing the noise of cable from your life.

Another huge expense are live events. It's definitely a thrill to go to your favorite band's concert or to a live sporting event, but you're probably paying a huge premium for that privilege. Instead of paying hundreds of dollars to see a famous band, look around for free concerts. Most communities have all kinds of options that you are already supporting with your tax dollars, from concerts to parks to museums to libraries. So take advantage of them!

Personally, I find the most entertainment from learning something new and making a lasting hobby out of it. Look into inexpensive classes near you or use the power of the Internet to learn something for free. If you choose the right hobbies, you could end up making money off of them. Hobbies have the ability to turn into money sinks or cash cows, so choose wisely! I will touch on some specific money saving and money making hobbies in a later chapter.

Recurring Expenses

Cable, Internet, phone bills, subscriptions. A lot of monthly costs are considered fixed and many people don't consider that they're paying way too much. Look at all of these very closely because most likely you can cut these too.

I already gave my advice on cutting cable, but if you can't live without it, at least take 10 minutes and call your cable provider to lower your monthly bill. Do a Google search and you will find scripts for how to lower you bill just by calling your provider and negotiating with them (i.e. threatening to cancel.) I have done this myself in my cable days and got it lowered every time. The last thing they want is for you to cancel. (In fact, they make it painfully difficult to do so.)

If you bundle your cable and Internet, even better. You can get the whole bundle lowered in one phone call. Add a note to your calendar to call your provider every six months to a year to get that bill lowered.

For your Internet, do *not* rent your modem from your cable company! It's a huge waste of money. Buy a modem and it will pay for itself many times over.

You are most likely paying too much for your phone bill, too. So many low cost providers exist today that the major carriers will have no choice pretty soon but to lower their costs. These low cost providers "piggyback" on one or more of the major networks, so find one that has good coverage in your area and be amazed at how much you can save! I personally use Republic Wireless, which piggybacks off of the Sprint network.

Clothing

Departments stores are constantly luring in customers with new "sales." Every week is a sale! A lot of us take the bait and end up owning an outfit for every day of the year, then we never wear most of them.

Instead, come up with a wardrobe where you can mix and match tops and bottoms and minimize the number of articles you need to buy. And try avoiding the department stores and going to discount stores like Marshalls instead. Buy last season's fashion. Go hunting at a thrift store. Buy used on eBay.

There are so many deals out there, so *please* never pay retail for clothing. And learn to reduce your dependence on constantly buying more clothing. There's no reason why you can't find some good quality outfits that you can wear for years. So what if you don't have the latest season's fashion? You can still look great buying clothes from a thrift store or clearance rack. And if your friends really care that much about your fashion sense, you need new friends.

Health Care

I consider health insurance as a necessary evil. Sure, there are millions of Americans getting away with not having it, but being the risk averse person that I am, I would rather not take the chance. One major expense could wipe out everything you've worked to achieve.

I remain hopeful that something will give when it comes to the ludicrous costs we currently have in the United States. Luckily, we continue to have more plan options to choose from, but you can still expect to get raked over the coals if you have any type of medical procedure. The best thing you can do to reduce health care costs is to eat healthy and stay active.

If you're in good health, a high deductible plan is your best option. With many high deductible plans you can also open a Health Savings Account (HSA) and sock away money tax free. Talk to your employer about whether you have this option, or check your retirement plan's website.

Key Takeaways

Now that you're tracking expenses, it's imperative to look at ways to reduce your costs in each of your major categories. There are always ways to save money when you put in the effort. It just takes commitment and forming habits.

Focus on one category at a time. You should most likely start with your food budget since there is almost always money to be saved there. Start eating out less and less. Learn to cook.

From there, you can move on to the next category that is breaking your budget. And so on. Don't get overwhelmed! Take it one category at a time and you will start developing lifelong cost cutting habits in no time.

GET RICH ACTION PLAN

Avoid the trap of getting a deal just for the sake of getting a deal. If you buy that $100 shirt for $40, ask yourself if you need that shirt in the first place. By following the advice in the previous chapter, you will start to question every purchase you make and find yourself much less influenced by the "I need it now" consumer culture in today's world.

At the end of this book, I included a link to the free guide, "27 Ways I Slashed My Budget by $1818 per Month." In this guide I go into more specifics of how I was able to save hundreds of thousands of dollars in just 6 years working a middle class job.

Now that you are spending so much less, it's time to invest that boatload of cash that's sitting in the bank! It's time to take a closer look at the wonderful world of investing.

5 INVEST THE SURPLUS

Savings Accounts

So you're making more, spending less, and growing that pile of money in your checking account. Now it's time to get a separate savings account where you can have extra cash for emergencies.

Your checking account should contain enough to pay your regular bills and the rest should be transferred into savings. You should grow your savings account to about 6 months worth of expenses in case crap hits the fan.

Many banks have signing bonuses where they actually *pay* you to create an account and maintain a certain balance at their bank. So shop around and see what branches are near you and what they offer. Chase Bank tends to have really good signup bonuses.

You can also go with an online banker like Ally.com, which is what I use. The only downside I have found with Ally is you can't deposit cash into your account since there are no physical locations. It does offer one of the best annual yields for a savings account, but rates on savings accounts in the U.S. are so ridiculously low these days that it really doesn't matter much, especially if you can get a great signup bonus. My Ally savings account yields 1% annual interest, and that is way above average in the United States.

Investment Accounts

Now that you have 6 months of expenses in your savings account, here comes the real fun – investing all that extra cash! In this chapter I'll be covering what accounts you can open and use to invest. In the next chapter I will go over what your portfolio should look like.

Don't worry – it's extremely simple. Billions of dollars are at stake, so financial institutions want you to think it's some complicated subject that requires more than a few chapters in an eBook.

Investing certainly *can* be more complicated if you want to turn it into a serious hobby, but to be successful requires very little effort and time commitment. I'm here to show you how to make the right investment decisions now so you can let your money work for you on autopilot.

401(k) or 403(b)

If you have a 401(k) or 403(b), you will want to start there. Depending on your employer's plan, you may or may not have a certain percentage matched. You definitely want to take advantage of matching! It's free money your employer is contributing to your retirement account.

As of 2016, you can contribute up to $18,000 per year of your own paycheck into your account, which will reduce your taxable income and grow tax free until retirement. The one downside to these plans is that they have limited options for what you can invest in, but I still recommend putting as much as possible into it up to the contribution limit.

Individual retirement accounts (IRA)

If you still have more to invest, your next option is opening an Individual Retirement Account (IRA). You won't have a choice with your 401(k) provider, but you can use any number of companies to establish your IRA. I recommend Vanguard for reasons we will go over in the next chapter.

You can open either a Roth or Traditional IRA. With a Roth IRA, you pay taxes up front on what you contribute, but pay no taxes in retirement. A traditional IRA is similar to a 401(k) where you are making a "tax-deferred" contribution, meaning your taxable income is reduced in the contribution year and you pay taxes when you withdraw.

Obviously, your goal is to pay as little in taxes as possible, whether that is today or in the future. It's difficult to project whether you will make more money today or when you are retired, but most likely you will be living a frugal lifestyle in your retirement and your income will be lower.

I use a Traditional IRA for this reason. As of 2016, the IRA contribution limit is $5,500 ($6,500 for those age 50 or over).

You will also want to check that your Modified Adjusted Gross Income (MAGI) is not too high, depending on your filing status. You can find this all on the IRS website or with a Google search of "IRA MAGI limits." (It's a good problem to have if you make more than the income limit!)

Health Savings Accounts (HSA)

Finally, you might also have access to a health savings account (HSA) through your employer, which is yet another way to invest tax-free for your retirement.

An HSA is a tax-advantaged account available to those enrolled in a high-deductible plan. With an HSA, you contribute funds tax-free that can be used any time for qualified medical expenses.

But guess what? There is no rule stating you *have* to use those funds for medical expenses. In other words, you can withdraw the funds after retirement just like a traditional IRA.

Some employers will even contribute a certain dollar amount to your HSA when you open one. It's free money!

Depending on your HSA plan, your investment options could be limited, and your account could get charged monthly fees. Check the rules and fee structure of your HSA provider.

Make sure to review any laws for the current year. Contribution limits and withdrawal age requirements are subject to change. At the time of this writing, HSA funds can be withdrawn penalty free at age 65, versus 59.5 for an IRA.

Brokerage Accounts

Once you've maxed out your retirement accounts, you can look into opening a brokerage account, which is just a normal investment account with no tax advantages. Once again, I recommend using Vanguard, and I'll tell you why in the next chapter.

If you're saving enough to get to this step, you are doing great! Invest every last dollar into this account that is not claimed by your checking account, emergency fund, or other retirement accounts. You won't have to wait until retirement to withdraw these funds, but you will be taxed on the capital gains. That's why I advise a "buy and hold" strategy, which I'll cover in the next chapter.

Key Takeaways

Investing is simple once you get the order down of what accounts to use. By going in this order, you will reduce your taxes and grow your money much faster into retirement. It is amazing how much difference this can make over the long term due to the power of compound interest!

1) Start by putting money into a savings account. While you will make very little on interest, you *need* an emergency fund of six months living expenses in case you lose your job or your income drops dramatically.

2) Next, invest in your 401(k) or 403(b). Your employer might match a certain percentage. If so, invest at least up to the matching amount. You can put up to $18,000 per year into this account if you want, or you can just

invest up to the matching amount and use an IRA for any additional funds you have.

3) Next, open an IRA. You will most likely want a Traditional IRA. Invest as much as you can into that account, up to $5,500 per year. That limit is always changing, so stay up to date on the tax laws each year to see if you can contribute more.

4) After that, you can use an HSA as an investment account if you have access to one. Check with your employer and your health insurance options. If an HSA is right for you, contribute as much as you are allowed into this account.

5) Finally, create a brokerage account if you have even more funds to invest. There are no tax advantages to a brokerage account, which is why you should do this step last.

Now that you have the order down of what accounts you should be using, I'll show you in the next chapter *exactly* where to invest your money for great returns and peace of mind. You'll be amazed how simple it is!

6 THE KISS PRINCIPLE

Disclaimer: This chapter is intended for informational purposes only, and represents the author's own opinions. Please conduct your own research before making any investment decisions. Past stock performance is no guarantee of future returns.

Keep It Simple

It seems like with the more information we continue to have available, the more complicated everything becomes. Don't get me wrong, I love having vast amount of information at my fingertips, but it's very easy to get sucked into the vortex and not know what advice to take.

In most areas of life, I subscribe to the KISS Principle (Keep It Simple, Stupid). Investing is no different.

The banks and financial institutions want us to believe investing is extremely complicated so that we fork over all power to them and get charged a hefty fee for it. But as I'll show you in this chapter, creating a portfolio is very easy for the average investor, and once set up it is truly one of the best passive income streams you can create for yourself.

Set up your portfolio the right way from the beginning, and you'll barely need to spend any time or money maintaining it. Remember to KISS it, set it, and forget it!

The Global Economy

It is an exciting time to be an investor with many emerging countries growing at such rapid rates, and a diversified portfolio will allow you to invest in those countries, either directly or indirectly. As long as the governments of the world don't screw things up, the global economy will continue to grow and create wealth, which creates wealth for you the investor!

You might think it wise to take an ethical stance against globalization because of exploited workers or the outsourcing of jobs. While these issues do exist, I don't think refusing to invest is the right answer.

Right or wrong, everything comes back to supply and demand. There is little demand for more expensively produced American made goods, so many manufacturing jobs have been outsourced to China and India. And while working conditions might not be the greatest in those countries, I think we will see improvements as we continue to invest in those countries and encourage their growth by being part owners in their businesses.

I am hopeful that worker rights will continue to improve as these countries continue to reap the rewards of participating in the global economy.

With that Public Service Announcement out of the way, let's get to the real meat of this chapter. How should you set up your investments? You will be amazed how easy it is!

Index Funds: The Holy Grail

When I refer to investing throughout this chapter, I am talking mainly about stocks and bonds because that is everything the average investor needs in his or her portfolio. That's it.

Obviously, there are other types of investments, like gold, real estate, and newer avenues such as Prosper and Lending Club. I will cover these briefly later in this chapter, but they really aren't necessary for a healthy portfolio. If you are passionate about investing and want to learn more, these can definitely be included in your portfolio in the future if you want to diversify more.

The reason stocks and bonds are all you need is because of the power of an investment called the index fund. Much like a typical mutual fund, an index fund allows you to invest in a large portion of the economy.

But unlike actively managed mutual funds, index funds are *passively managed*. What does this mean? The fund tracks a certain market index, such as the S&P 500 or the total world stock market. There is no team of analysts trying to decide where to allocate funds. All the manager of an index fund needs to do is mirror the performance of whatever index the fund is tracking.

Since there is very little management, you pay next to nothing in fees when owning an index fund! That means you reap nearly 100% of the rewards each and every year when you invest in an index fund!

The way fees work in a typical mutual fund, you have to pay a certain percentage to pay for transaction costs, advisory fees, marketing fees, and more. These percentages are often shown as an *expense ratio*, which is the total cost you pay to the fund divided by the total investment you have in the company.

For a mutual fund, the expense ratio can be anywhere from 1 to 2%. For an index fund, it drops to 0.1 or 0.2%, sometimes even lower. You might be thinking paying 1 or 2% is no big deal. You're still keeping 98% of your investment each year, right? Let's take a look at an example.

According to Vanguard (http://vgi.vg/1PlNuCw), the average expense ratio of a Vanguard index fund is 0.18%, and the industry average expense ratio is 1.01%. Even this small difference will produce a significant difference over time. Assuming identical 6% returns, a $50,000 initial investment will generate $15,109 in fees over 30 years compared to $75,394 for the average mutual fund, over a $60,000 difference!

You might be thinking, "That's great, but a mutual fund will actively manage my money and therefore make wiser decisions, so in the long run I'll make more." While some savvy mutual funds are able to consistently outperform the market, in most cases it simply does not happen.

A recent study from Portfolio Solutions and Betterment showed that index fund portfolios outperformed actively managed portfolios 82 to 90% of the time! Simply put, it is almost always more beneficial to use an index fund.

While a select few have shown they can beat the market year after year (e.g. Warren Buffet), the deck is stacked against you. And if a mutual fund actually *has* outperformed the market each of the last five years, how likely is it that they will continue to do so?

Odds are once you find a "successful" mutual fund, you already missed out on its glory days, so once you get in, you'll end up seeing below average returns. So put your money in an index fund, set it and forget it! Read on to find out how!

Vanguard

In case you haven't guessed it by now, my favorite investment company is Vanguard. The company continues to lead the charge of low cost investing and is credited as the first to offer the index fund to individual investors.

It is very easy to create an account and get started there – just go to Vanguard.com. From there, you can open an IRA, a brokerage account, or transfer existing accounts. And it's all free! (Refer back to the previous chapter for the order you should open and invest in your accounts. Remember, you won't have a choice on what company to use for your 401(k). Your employer chooses.)

(*Note*: There are minimum dollar values you must invest in order to purchase many of the index funds offered by Vanguard. At the time of this writing, most index funds require a minimum of $3,000 to invest.)

Once you have your account set up, you link to your checking or savings account and start investing!

Other Investment Companies

There are hundreds of companies that will gladly invest your money. I am only going to focus on Vanguard and the funds it has available, but the principles are the same no matter what company you are looking to use to house your investments.

Some of the big names that I have personally used and like are Vanguard, Fidelity, and Scottrade. They each have low transaction costs and plenty of low cost fund options. There are obviously many others besides these, so no matter who you decide to go with, make sure they have plenty of options for low cost index funds.

Whatever you do, do *not* get sucked into a high cost actively managed mutual fund! This is a recipe for wealth destruction.

The Perfect Portfolio

So now that you have your account set up, where should your money go? There are really only three index funds you need. It's that simple. Here is the perfect portfolio.

Vanguard Total Bond Market Index Fund (VBMFX): From Vanguard's website, "the fund invests about 30% in corporate bonds and 70% in U.S. government bonds of all maturities (short-, intermediate-, and long-term issues)." In other words, investing in this one fund is all you need to be properly diversified in the bond market!

Vanguard Total Stock Market Index Fund (VTSMX): From Vanguard's website, "Vanguard Total Stock Market Index Fund is designed to provide investors with exposure to the entire U.S. equity market, including small-, mid-, and large-cap growth and value stocks. The fund's key attributes are its low costs, broad diversification, and the potential for tax efficiency. Investors looking for a low-cost way to gain broad exposure to the U.S. stock market who are willing to accept the volatility that comes with stock market investing may wish to consider this fund as either a core equity holding or your only domestic stock fund." In other words, investing in this one fund is all you need to do to be properly diversified in the U.S. stock market!

Vanguard Total International Stock Index Fund (VGTSX): From Vanguard's website, "This fund offers investors a low cost way to gain equity exposure to both developed and emerging international economies. The fund tracks stock markets all over the globe, with the exception of the United States. Because it invests in non-U.S. stocks, including those in developed and emerging markets, the fund can be more volatile than a domestic fund. Long-term investors who want to add a diversified international equity position to their portfolio might want to consider this fund as an option." In other words, investing in this one fund is all you need to be properly diversified in the international stock market!

So, what percentage of your investments should be in each of these? That depends on your risk tolerance.

Many investors just put one-third into each of the above three index funds and call it a day. Others put a higher percentage into the stock funds because they have a higher risk tolerance.

Generally speaking, the younger you are, the more you should put into stocks because you have decades to go until you need that money. Bonds are considered the safer investment, so as you get older you will want to move more into bonds.

One rule of thumb is to put your age as a percentage into bonds and the rest into stocks. Therefore, if you are 25, you would put 25% into the Total Bond Market Fund and split the remaining 75% into your other two funds.

Okay, so you've bought these three funds, now what? That's it! Really? Yes! All that's left for you to do is continue to contribute to these funds each month and to rebalance two to four times per year.

Rebalancing means looking at the values in each of your index funds either quarterly or a couple times per year and transferring money among the three so that you are back to the right percentages.

As an example, if the stock market outperforms the bond market, your 75% investment in stocks might turn into 80% at the end of the year. You would want to move 5% of that back into bonds to get back to your 75/25 balance.

Why? Because you don't want to be "overweight" in one fund, especially when that fund has been doing really well.

The market has a tendency of correcting itself, so you do not want to be too heavily invested in stocks only for the stock market to come crashing down.

In other words, do not put all of your eggs in one basket. Rebalance every quarter and you will be just fine. With a portfolio this simple, it will take all of 5 minutes!

A Note on Your 401(k)

If you are investing in your 401(k), you probably won't have these index funds as a choice. You will probably have some kind of Target Retirement Funds to choose from.

Instead of just picking the fund closest to your target retirement date, look at the *Prospectus* of each one to see what percentage is invested into stocks and bonds.

For example, if you want to invest 75% into stocks and 25% into bonds, find the Target Retirement Fund that comes closest to that mix. Ignore the year. I am invested in a 2025 Retirement fund because it is about 75/25 stocks to bonds. I doubt I will retire by age 39, but one can hope!

Other Investments

Investing is so easy, it's almost boring! If you want it to be a more involved hobby, it certainly can be. If you think you can do better than these funds through other avenues, have at it, but I would start small. Put aside 5 or 10% of your investments for these alternatives to see if you have any success.

Individual Stocks

Investing in individual stocks is one way to make investing into a fun hobby. Find a company that you think is poised to do well over the next 5-10 years and you could vastly outperform the market if you choose wisely.

Many "investors" speculate by buying and selling constantly for the short term, but you'll end up paying higher taxes and more transaction costs. My advice is to find a good company or two that have long term growth potential, buy and hold, and set and forget.

Remember that stocks are part ownership in a business. Would you want to buy a company that is loaded with debt and does not have a sustainable business model?

Real Estate

You can also invest in real estate if you have the itch to diversify more. Many people have made lots of money in real estate, but just like any investment, you should look at it from a long term perspective. Are you buying in a desirable location that won't crash and burn (i.e. like the 2007 bubble)?

The beauty of being a landlord is you can collect a monthly rent check for little to no work if you know what you're doing. Real estate investing is beyond the scope of this book, but it can be a great way to supplement your income and diversify your portfolio. For simpler real estate investment options, consider investing in a Real Estate Investment Trust (REIT). Vanguard even has a REIT index fund (VGSIX).

Precious Metals

What about precious metals like gold and silver? Many advocates of gold investing have legitimate concerns that it's only a matter of time before a global currency crisis will leave hard assets like gold and silver as the currency of choice.

True, gold and silver have been used as currency in the past, and they very well could be used as currency again in the future. But I strongly believe the best investments are in businesses that are consistently creating value and solving problems for customers each and every year.

Lending Club and Prosper

Finally, I know a lot of people who have had success on Lending Club and Prosper. These are peer-to-peer lending services where you can provide capital to individual borrowers and reap the rewards from the interest earned.

According to Lending Club, investors have averaged between a 6 and 9% return, which isn't too shabby if you ask me. With the proper research, both of these services would make great options to dabble further into your investing hobby.

Just to reiterate , I recommend keeping your initial investment small and putting at least 80 to 90% of your hard earned portfolio into tried and true index funds.

(*Note*: Prosper and Lending Club are not available in some states.)

Key Takeaways

Investing is extremely easy with index funds. You only need three funds for long term success: VBMFX, VTSMX, and VGTSX. These three funds will give you all the diversification you need into the stock and bond markets.

Vanguard makes it very simple to link to your bank accounts and start investing. If you have money to invest, get going. Open an account today!

Disclosure: I am long VBMFX, VTSMX, and VGTSX. This chapter expresses my own opinions. I am not receiving compensation for it other than from the royalties from selling this book.

7 BUILD THE SNOWBALL

We are lucky to live in such an age of abundance that it has become so easy to save money. On the flip side, our consumer culture has made it just as easy to spend money. It all boils down to this: do you value freedom or your possessions more?

The more you spend, the more you need to work to pay for it all. The more you have to work, the less free time you have. Once you realize this, you will become addicted to building your wealth to escape this rat race.

There are really only two ways to build your wealth: you can increase your income, or you can cut your expenses. I have already touched on these subjects in earlier chapters, but they bear repeating.

Increasing your income and reducing expenses are so important to accelerating your financial independence that I decided to devote a chapter to even more tips you can implement today that will pay dividends for the rest of your life.

At this point, you should be well on your way to financial independence, but you can use the tips in this chapter to get there even quicker!

Increase Your Income

As I said earlier, money does not buy happiness. It buys time. The more money you make now, the more time you will have in the future to do whatever you want. If you still want to work, great, but you won't *have* to work. That is the point of this book – show that you can be free to live however you want much quicker than you were led to believe.

One way to do that is increasing your income today. You might be qualified for a promotion or there might be another company across town that pays more. Whatever the case, if you think that higher paying job would be worth your time and effort, go for it!

If you are already dissatisfied with your career path, you might want to look at a completely different career. Whatever the case, there is always money to be made if you put yourself out there. Even if you don't like your current path, since you're on the fast track to financial independence it won't be long until you have enough "FU" money to get out and do something else! That's the beauty of this whole philosophy.

Aside from your job, there are other ways to make money on the side, and they can even be fun hobbies.

Side Hustles

A lot of people have second jobs out of necessity. Even if you don't *need* a second income, I always recommend you look at other avenues for side money, especially if they allow you the freedom to spend as much or as little time as you want on them! Here are some common side hustles that can make you money in your free time.

Uber: More and more cities are offering Uber and it's very easy to become a driver. You can turn the service on and become a driver as much or as little as you want.

Tutoring: There are various tutoring services both online and in your community where you could make extra income. Think about what skills you have that you could teach to others. One that almost anyone could do is a service called NiceTalk (nicetalk.com), where you get paid to have English conversations with students trying to learn English.

Flipping: I have personally used this method for side income, and it's one of the easiest and most fun ways to make a few extra bucks. Buy items for cheap at yard sales, thrift shops, or wherever you can get them, and turn around and sell them for more on eBay, Amazon, or Craigslist. Buy low, sell high, that's all there is to it! There is a wealth of information on what and where to buy – check out the Reddit flipping community reddit.com/r/flipping for more details.

Digital Content: You can write an eBook like this one and get paid for it. If you have content to share with the world, why not make an eBook out of it? If you can string coherent sentences together about a topic you are interested in, you can write an eBook.

Or, you could start a blog and later write an eBook based on your blog posts. Or you could create a YouTube channel. However you want to do it, there is money to be made in publishing content online. The money varies widely depending on how big of an audience you build. It's all based on the effort you put into it. If it's something you would enjoy anyway, you might as well go for it. The extra income is just icing on the cake.

Consultant: If you have some kind of expertise, why not turn it into a side consulting business? You can probably charge more than what you make at your job, and you can take on as many or as few clients as you want.

If none of these appeal to you, there are many more options to choose from. It's all about just taking action. This is the most difficult part, because any side hustle is going to take up more of your precious time.

But given the choice between vegging out or making a few bucks, why not reward yourself with some hard work and new talents? And like I said, you can spend as much or as little time as you want on your side hustle – there won't be any bosses staring over your shoulder!

Cut Those Costs!

I know we already discussed the importance of cutting expenses in an earlier chapter, but I can't stress it enough! There are so many ways to save money with all the choices we have as consumers today. The key is buy what you need, not what other people think you need! Here are some more tips and tricks to save.

Buy High Quality

You might think buying quality items means you're paying more. In most cases, that's true up front, but think of it from a long term perspective. Would you rather spend $200 for a pair of work boots that will last you 10 years or spend $50 for boots that are going to wear out every single year? Personally, I would take the former any day. The same goes for all kinds of products – clothing, tools, electronics.

Sometimes the higher end product is very much worth the cost if the product is going to pay for itself many times over years down the road. In other cases, you're just paying for the brand name. Or, it's a product you don't need to last because you barely ever use it.

If you use a tool once a year, you don't need the most expensive, highest quality. But if you use it every week, you should look for something durable that you won't have to constantly replace.

Check out the Buy It For Life Reddit community reddit.com/r/buyitforlife to find those products that will last you a long time and save you money in the long run.

Buy Used

I talked about buying used in an earlier chapter, and I can't stress this enough. There are so many perfectly good used products in the world, yet we are always conditioned to go to the store and buy brand new.

Do me a favor and check your local thrift stores, search Craigslist, search eBay, and look at Used items on Amazon (yes, Amazon sells plenty of used products too!). Many times these items have barely been used and you can get them for half the cost of a new one. To me, that's a no brainer!

I buy used shoes and clothing at thrift stores and on eBay all the time. I have bought used furniture and appliances on Craigslist. And guess what? I have never had an issue with quality and I saved a ton of money in the process. The key is obviously doing your research and making sure you're getting something good.

The beauty of eBay and Amazon used products is you can see whether you are buying from a reputable seller. With Craigslist, you might be dealing with people who don't sell very often, but I have found that nearly everyone I have met on Craigslist ended up being very honest.

To avoid getting overwhelmed by the vast number of used goods available on these platforms, you can set up alerts for specific items you are interested in when they become available on eBay, Amazon, or Craigslist.

Say you are looking for a chest freezer on Craigslist. You can set up an email alert for the search term "chest freezer" and have the results delivered right to your inbox so you don't have to search numerous times a day.

The same goes for eBay and Amazon. You can "follow" a search on eBay and you can track products on Amazon through third party websites such as CamelCamelCamel.com. These will all deliver emails to your inbox when items come in stock at whatever price point you are looking for. That way you will never overpay again!

No More Impulse Buying!

Instead of deciding you want something, then buying it right away, try adding an item to a wish list or online shopping cart and waiting a month. If you still want it after a month, go ahead. Otherwise, delete it.

I have saved myself from buying something so many times by delaying a purchase. A month later I would realize I really didn't need that item. If you practice this method of delaying gratification, you will soon realize how little you actually need. As a result, your quality of life and bank account will skyrocket!

Fun and Cheap Hobbies

I touched on finding cheaper hobbies earlier, and I really stand by this. If you love a hobby but you're spending thousands of dollar per year on it, consider whether you are getting that much back in enjoyment or if there's a way to get that same enjoyment at a fraction of the cost. Just because all of your friends are constantly upgrading their equipment doesn't mean you have to. Don't give in to the peer pressure!

You can still enjoy a hobby without throwing all of your money away on it. Some cheap hobbies I have enjoyed over the years include camping, backpacking, cooking, writing, reading, volunteering, photography, bicycling, playing board games, and playing sports.

While some may have high upfront costs, these hobbies can all be done for very cheap in the long run if you are smart about your purchases. By all means, spend money on your passions and live life, but once you have what you need for your hobby, you don't need to keep buying all the best and newest gear! Save that money and let it grow so you have even more time to enjoy your passions in your early retirement.

And like I said before, hobbies can *make* you money, such as writing or blogging, or reselling items on eBay and Amazon. They can also save you money by teaching yourself DIY skills on YouTube. You would be amazed how easy some fixes are after watching a quick YouTube video! The possibilities for hobbies are endless, so find one you love that won't break the bank!

Key Takeaways

Find ways to increase your income and cut expenses even further to accelerate your route to financial freedom. Look to make more money at your job or take up a side hustle that will give you a little extra. Find hobbies that will save money or even make money for you.

Most importantly, have fun!

You don't have to be miserable to achieve financial independence at a young age. You just have to rethink the status quo consumer culture and turn it on its head.

You can take the frugal lifestyle to the extreme if you want, but keep reminding yourself to have fun! If at any point you're not enjoying the path to wealth, reevaluate what you're doing and keep moving toward your goals!

Nothing worth fighting for is ever easy, but it doesn't have to be miserable. So keep a smile on your face and stay positive. The best is yet to come!

8 LIVE YOUR DREAMS

We all have one life on this planet, one chance to live in accordance with our principles, our desires. You can make money, you can lose money, but you can't get back time. Your road to financial freedom will encounter its obstacles and its hardships, but everything worth fighting for has its challenges.

Let's recap the steps you can take over the next month to steer yourself toward financial freedom:

1) Write down your five year goals for what you want your life to look like. Exactly what are you hoping to accomplish? Revise every year or whenever your goals change. By taking the time to think about what you really want, you'll begin to realize how little you actually need to be happy.

2) Avoid debt. Focus on paying off credit cards and student loans. If you haven't gone to college yet, think twice about it or look for every way possible to minimize the cost. Avoid a mortgage until you *know* you are where you want to be. Buy a small house if you do end up buying. Less is more.

3) Track your finances. Use Mint or You Need a Budget. Look at everything monthly. Make a budget, but don't use it as an excuse to spend everything. Adjust your budget as life changes and as your philosophy on money changes. You might be able to get rid of it once your frugal habits starts running on autopilot.

4) Focus on cutting costs. Take one category at a time and slash it until you're comfortable with it, then move to the next category. Pretty soon thriftiness will become the norm.

5) Create an emergency fund of six month's expenses. Invest everything left over that isn't needed for monthly bills. Use accounts with tax advantages first so your wealth will compound even faster over time.

6) Use index funds and keep it simple. You only need three to have a

successful portfolio: VBMFX, VTSMX, and VGTSX.

7) Keep looking for ways to build your pile of money. Grow your income at work or with side hustles and cut your costs even more by finding cheaper hobbies. Make sure you're still having fun!

8) Live your dreams.

Once you build that stash of FU money, you'll find a huge weight has been lifted! Your time becomes more valuable and you spend it how *you* want and not how somebody else wants. You will become that much closer to realizing the ideal life you envisioned in Step 1. Financial freedom means absolute freedom!

You can do this. I have tried to show you with this book that it's not very hard! Everyone has different goals and dreams, but don't let finances get in the way of those. Take control of them today and you will be well on your way to a prosperous life.

I hope this book helped you understand that once you know what you want out of life, you will quickly realize how *little* material wealth you need to get there. You will not only spend less along the way, you will need less to really enjoy each day.

Your wealth will continue to snowball until you have everything you need and more to live a long, happy, free life. No more alarm clocks, no more bosses. Just absolute freedom to live the life you always dreamed!

Remember: time is our most precious resource. So get started on the path to freedom today!

TOOLS & RESOURCES

Here is a list of the links referred to throughout the book. I hope you find them useful in your journey to financial freedom!

- **NerdWallet.com** – Find a credit card for your needs.
- **Mint.com** – Free budgeting software.
- **You Need a Budget** (ynab.com) – Paid budgeting software.
- **AutoTempest.com** – Find great deals on used cars.
- **RepublicWireless.com** – Low cost cell phone provider.
- **Ally Bank** (ally.com) – Online banking solution.
- **Vanguard.com** – Discount broker with various low-cost index funds.
- **Scottrade.com** – A great discount broker for stock trading.
- **LendingClub.com** – Peer-to-peer lending service.
- **Prosper.com** – Another peer-to-peer lending service.
- **Uber.com** – Become a driver and make some side cash.
- **NiceTalk.com** – Become an English tutor in your free time.
- **Reddit.com/r/flipping** – Buy products for cheap, sell them for more.
- **Reddit.com/r/buyitforlife** – Buy high quality, durable, items.
- **CamelCamelCamel.com** – Track Amazon price changes.

SPECIAL BONUS

Congratulations! You're well on your way to financial freedom and a lifetime of riches. But I have so much more I want to share!

For starters, I created a free guide called 27 Ways I Slashed My Budget by $1818 per Month" This PDF includes 27 different cost cutting measures I have personally used to cut spending. These actionable tips and tricks will give you plenty of ideas to save even more money right away!

Visit the page below to get the free guide along with some other free goodies. You'll also receive exclusive updates every few weeks! Don't worry: I will never spam you or give out your email to anyone for any reason, and you can always unsubscribe at any time.

projectfreemind.com/subscribe

ABOUT THE AUTHOR

JAY TOMLINSON is an entrepreneur, former finance professional, and author of the FU Money Series. Jay became financially secure in his late 20's, affording him the ability to take time off of work to pursue his hobbies and passions. When he's not obsessing over financial independence, Jay can be found hiking in the woods, volunteering, or spending time with loved ones.

Join his mailing list at projectfreemind.com/subscribe to get his FREE guide "27 Ways I Slashed My Budget By $1818 Per Month."

Get in touch with Jay on his website ProjectFreeMind.com or his author page TomlinsonBooks.com. You can also follow Jay on Twitter @tomlinsonbooks. He would love to hear from you!

www.ingramcontent.com/pod-product-compliance
Lightning Source LLC
Chambersburg PA
CBHW071018250225

22520CB00024B/271